WORLD ABOUT US

WIND & WATER POWER

CLINT TWIST

GLOUCESTER PRESS

London New York Toronto Sydney

© Aladdin Books Ltd 1992

Designed and produced by
Aladdin Books Ltd
28 Percy Street
London W1P 9FF

First published in
Great Britain in 1992 by
Franklin Watts Ltd
96 Leonard Street
London EC2A 4RH

Design: David West
          Children's
          Book Design
Designer: Stephen
          Woosnam-Savage
Editor: Fiona Robertson
Consultant: Brian Price,
          Pollution Consultant
Illustrator: Mike Lacy

Printed in Belgium
A CIP catalogue record for this
book is available from the
British Library.

ISBN 0 7496 0802 1

Contents

Introduction

The natural forces of wind and water have long been used to provide energy for windmills and sailing ships. Today that energy can be converted into electricity. Producing electricity from wind and water requires a strong, steady flow. Water can be made to flow along channels and pipes, or stored behind dams. Wind, however, cannot be relied on to provide a steady flow of energy, and is more difficult to harness.

Why alternative energy?

Each year, the world uses more and more energy, especially in the form of electricity. Most of the world's electricity is made by power stations that burn fossil fuels – coal, oil and gas. Some electricity is also produced by nuclear fuel. These types of fuel produce pollution and are becoming more expensive. Wind and water power offer cleaner sources of energy that will never run out.

Coal, oil and gas are non-renewable energy sources. When they run out, they can never be replaced. Supplies of oil, for example, are expected to run out in about 50 years.

Oil slicks spilled by tankers are deadly to marine life.

When fossil fuels are burned, they give off the gases carbon dioxide and water vapour. If too many of these gases enter the atmosphere, they can cause temperatures to rise. This is called global warming.

The waste from nuclear fuel remains dangerous for thousands of years. It is difficult to dispose of safely and must be transported in protective casks to prevent any leaks.

The wind

The wind is a powerful source of free energy.
People have used wind power for
thousands of years. The wind enabled ships
to sail the sea long before engines were
invented. On land, windmills were used
to provide a slow turning movement for
grinding corn. Traditional windmills
were made of wood and cloth, and
their sails could be adjusted according
to the speed of the wind.

Sailing ships and barges use
carefully arranged sets of sails
to gather energy from the wind.

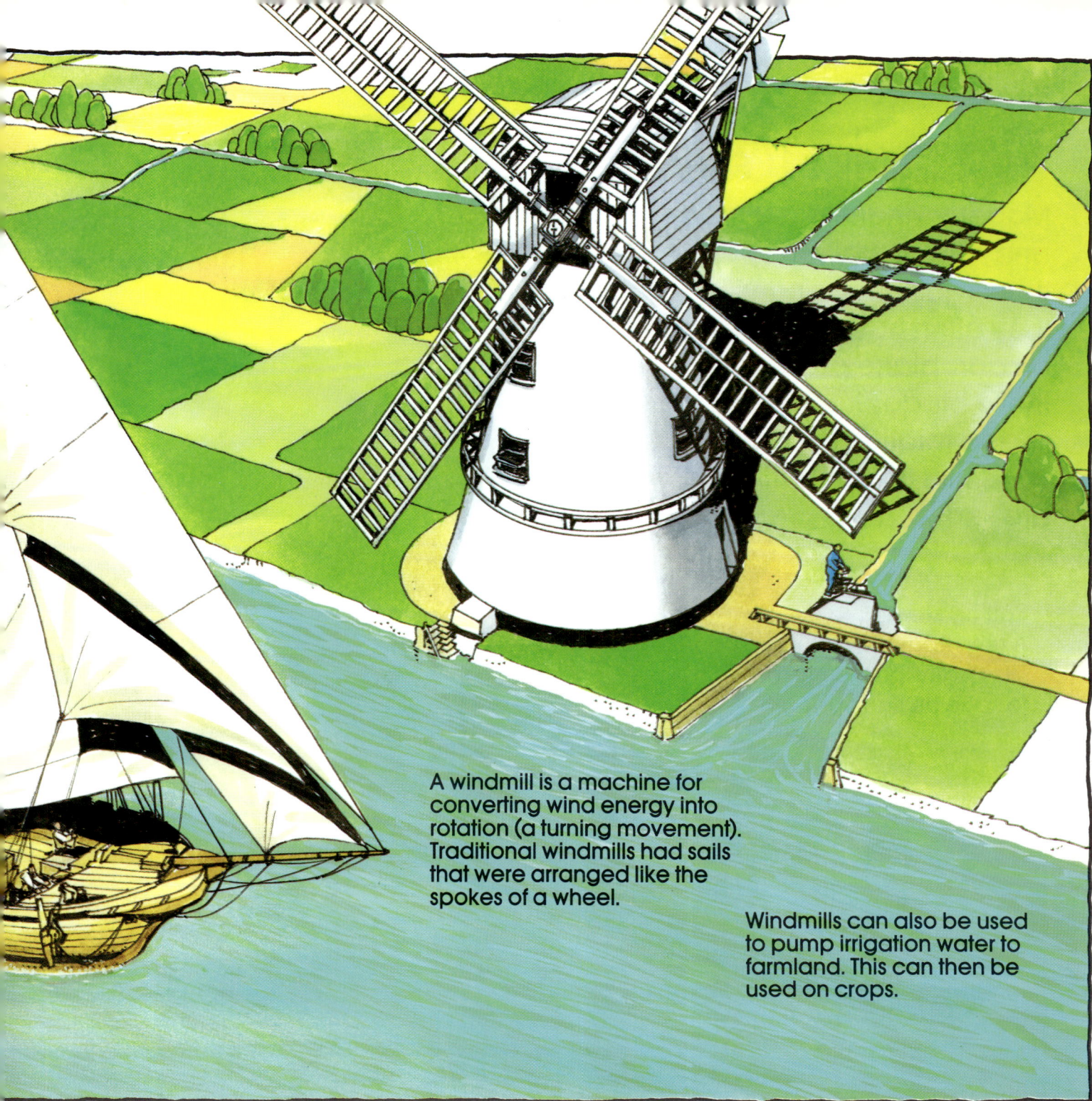

A windmill is a machine for converting wind energy into rotation (a turning movement). Traditional windmills had sails that were arranged like the spokes of a wheel.

Windmills can also be used to pump irrigation water to farmland. This can then be used on crops.

Wind power

Modern windmills are made from concrete and steel. Usually they are much bigger than traditional windmills. Instead of sails they often have blades shaped like those of an aeroplane propeller. The wind makes these blades turn at high speed. This high-speed rotation is used to make electricity. Windmills that are built to produce electricity are known as wind turbines.

Sailing ships
A few modern ships have been fitted with lightweight metal sails to save on fuel costs.

The turbine's spinning blades turn a driveshaft connected to a generator – a machine that converts rotation into electricity.

The top of the wind turbine can be turned on its tower, so that the blades always face straight into the wind.

Engineers try out different wind turbine designs. Some have hinged blades, while others have blades mounted on a vertical driveshaft.

Generator

Gears

Driveshaft

Turning mechanism

Blade

Tower windmill

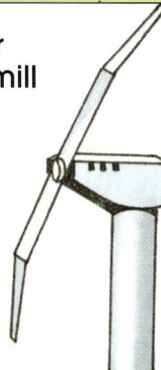

Vertical axis windmill

Darrieus

The shape of the blades on the Darrieus wind turbine allow it to operate whichever direction the wind is blowing.

9

Wind farms

Instead of building one big wind turbine, it is often cheaper to build lots of small ones. These are set out on wind farms. A large wind farm can produce enough electricity to supply a city. Wind farms have to be built where the wind blows strongest, usually on hills and mountains. Power cables carry the electricity down to towns and cities. However, ways of storing the electricity must be found for days when there is no wind.

A wind farm takes up a large area of land and can be very ugly. However, most wind farms are built in remote areas where the land is not much use for anything else.

The biggest wind farms already in use are in California, USA.

Hundreds of spinning turbines can be very noisy. The turbines can also cause television interference. The broadcast signals bounce off the turbine's blades.

Water power

A windmill takes energy from the movement of air. In the same way, a waterwheel takes energy from moving water. The flow of the water pushes against the wheel and makes it rotate. A waterwheel can be built wherever there is a suitable river or stream. In ancient times, waterwheels were used to grind corn. Later, waterwheels drove machines in the first factories.

Water was guided to the waterwheel along a channel called a "race".

Types of waterwheel
Waterwheels are one of the oldest mechanical inventions. In an overshot wheel, the water is channelled over the wheel to fall on blades at the front. In an undershot wheel, the water falls on blades at the back and then flows beneath the wheel.

Undershot wheel

Overshot wheel

The wheel was made of wood or metal. The water pushed against a series of blades fitted around the rim of the wheel.

Watermills were once a familiar sight in many parts of the world. Today, some places still have working waterwheels.

Stopping the flow

The movement of water is much easier to control than the movement of air. The flow of rivers and streams can be stopped by building a dam. The best place to build a dam is across a steep-sided river valley. Behind the dam, the water collects into an artificial lake called a reservoir. A steady flow of water can then be channelled away from the reservoir when it is needed.

Building the dam
Before work can begin, the flow of the river must be stopped by a temporary dam otherwise the area would be flooded. Dams are built to stop flooding, to provide irrigation water, and to produce electricity.

The deeper the water stored behind the dam, the greater the amount of energy it can produce. This stored energy is called a "head of water".

One of the main uses of reservoirs is to provide a steady supply of water to houses and factories.

Dams

A dam needs to be very strong to hold back all the water in the reservoir. The top of the dam is quite narrow. Below the water, however, the base of the dam is much thicker. The first dams were simply big walls with sloping sides, and were made of rocks and soil. Modern dams are usually built of concrete reinforced with steel. Many dams curve in one direction, because a curved shape is much stronger than a straight wall.

An embankment dam has a core of broken rock and sloping sides made of soil and clay. A buttressed dam is supported by buttresses at the front. An arch dam has a strong curved shape. In a double curvature dam, the dam curves in two directions.

Embankment dam

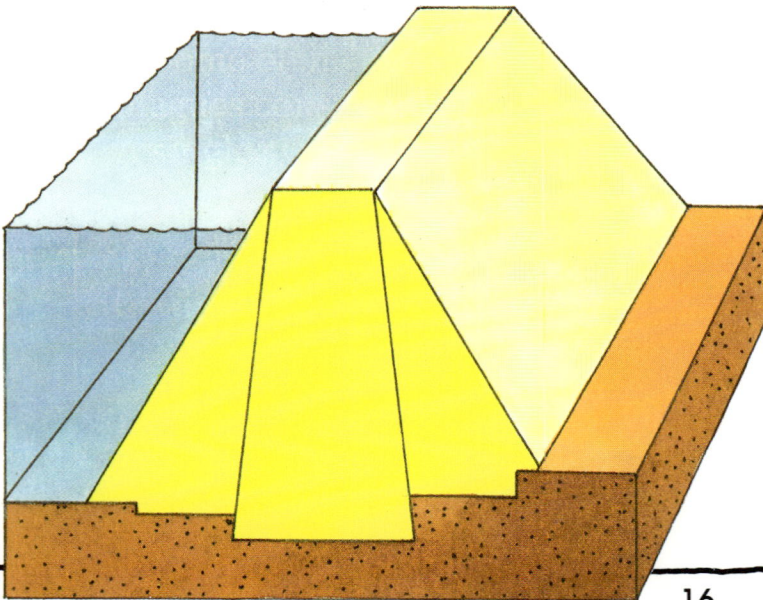

Buttressed straight dam

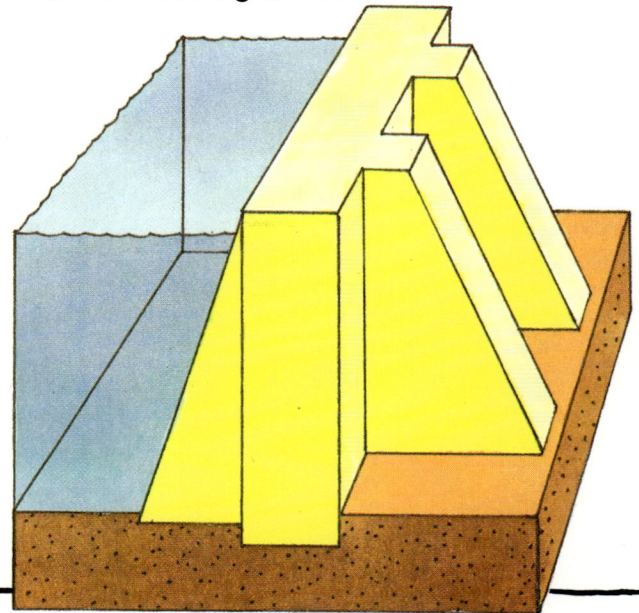

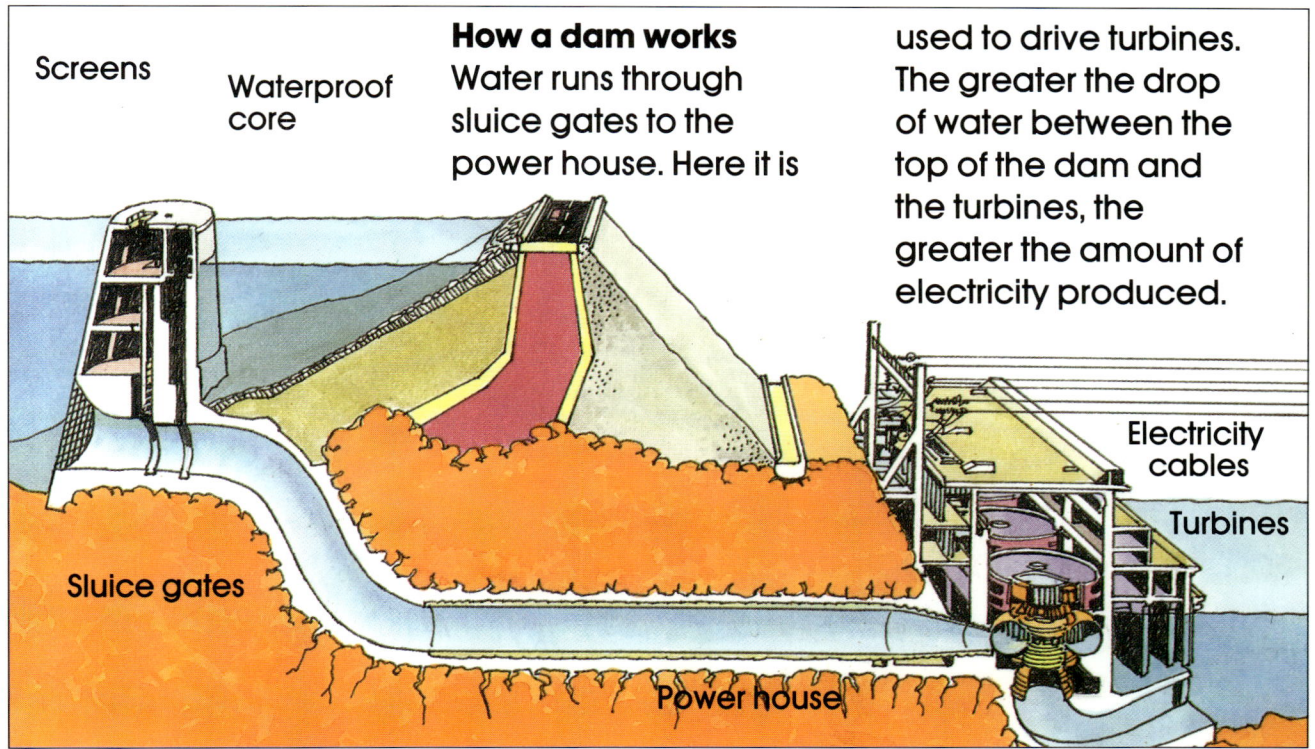

Screens

Waterproof core

How a dam works
Water runs through sluice gates to the power house. Here it is used to drive turbines. The greater the drop of water between the top of the dam and the turbines, the greater the amount of electricity produced.

Sluice gates

Electricity cables

Turbines

Power house

Arch dam

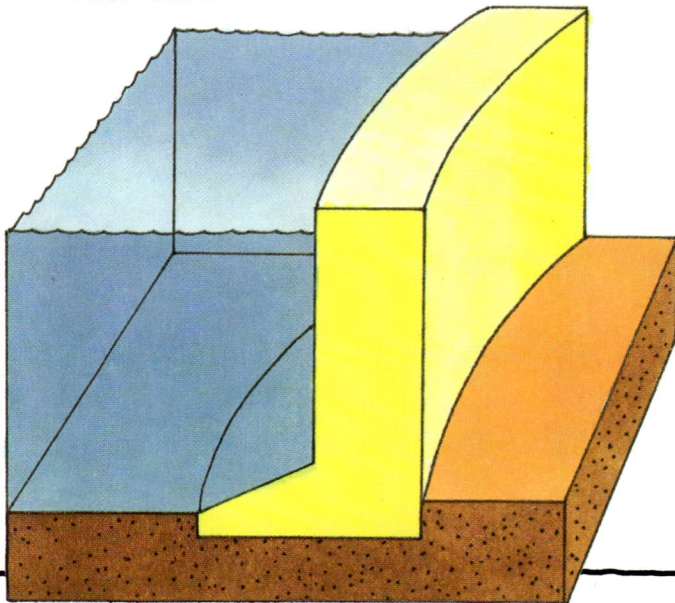

Double curvature dam

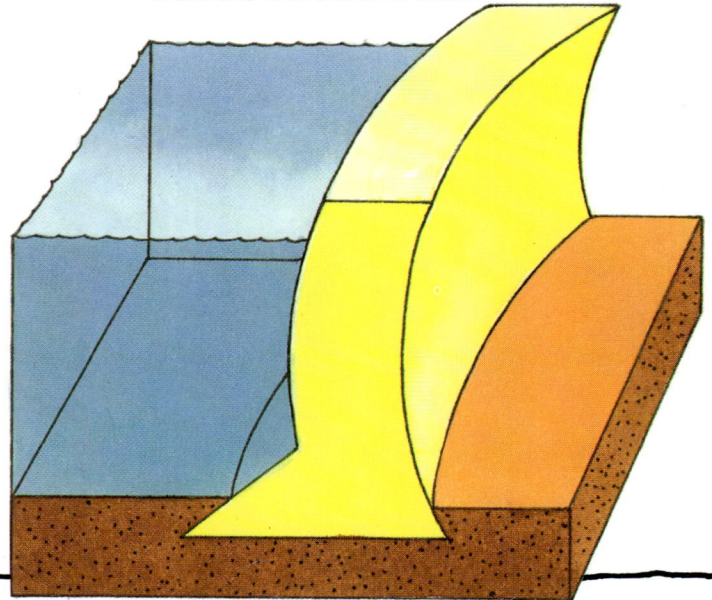

Generating electricity

Electricity produced by water power is called hydro-electricity. Water from behind the dam is channelled down through pipes. As the water flows downwards it gains energy. At the end of the pipes are several water turbines. A water turbine works in the same way as a waterwheel, but can turn much faster. The shaft of each turbine is connected to an electrical generator.

Inside each electrical generator are magnets surrounded by thousands of coils of wire. The movement of the turbines makes the magnets spin. This creates electricity in the coils of wire.

The Francis reaction turbine is immersed in the flow of water.

The Pelton wheel impulse turbine is driven by a jet of water and needs a powerful flow.

The Kaplan axial flow turbine is used when the flow is not very strong.

Generators are usually mounted above the turbines in a room called the generator hall. The electricity produced is carried away in cables.

The water in the top reservoir represents stored electricity.

The environment
The Dinorwic power station in North Wales was built underground so as not to spoil the landscape. Thousands of metres of tunnel had to be carved through solid rock.

The surge hole acts like a giant overflow pipe.

Storing power

Water can also be used to store electricity. Two reservoirs are needed, one higher up than the other. During the day, when the demand for power is high, water from the top reservoir flows down huge pipes to turbines. At night, when demand is low, spare electricity is used to pump water back up to the top reservoir. The next day, the same water can be used to produce electricity again.

The power station works 24 hours a day. The storage system works because less electricity is needed at night (off-peak hours) than during the day (peak hours).

The two-reservoir system used at Dinorwic power station is called a "pumped storage" system.

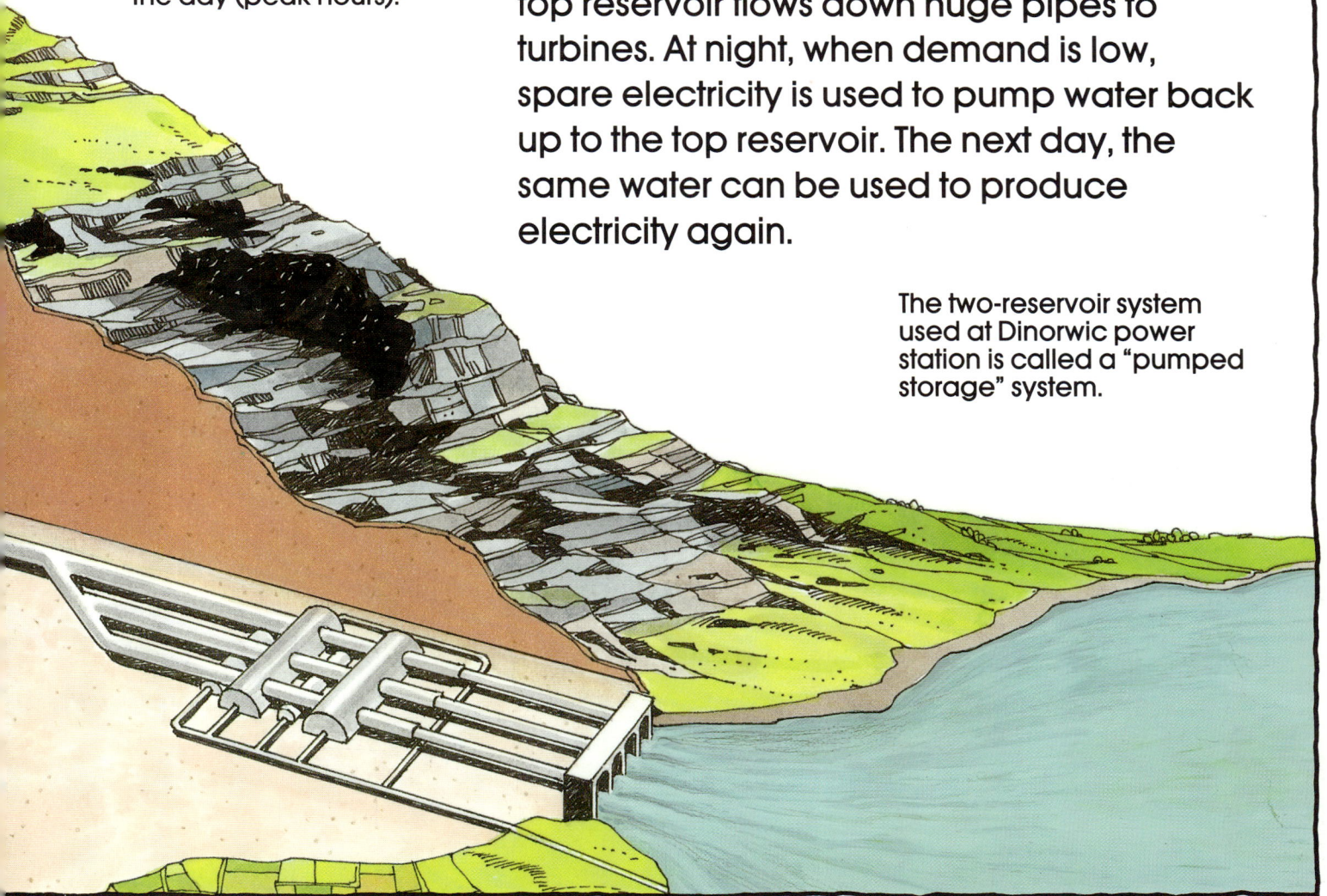

The problems

Hydro-electricity is a renewable source of energy that does not cause pollution, but it can create some problems. Hydro-electric power stations are often built in the steep-sided valleys of mountainous regions. Building a dam means flooding the upper part of a valley to create the reservoir. People and animals that once lived in the valley have to find somewhere else to live.

The Itaipu Dam in Amazonia flooded over 120,000 hectares of forest. Over 50,000 people were forced to leave the area.

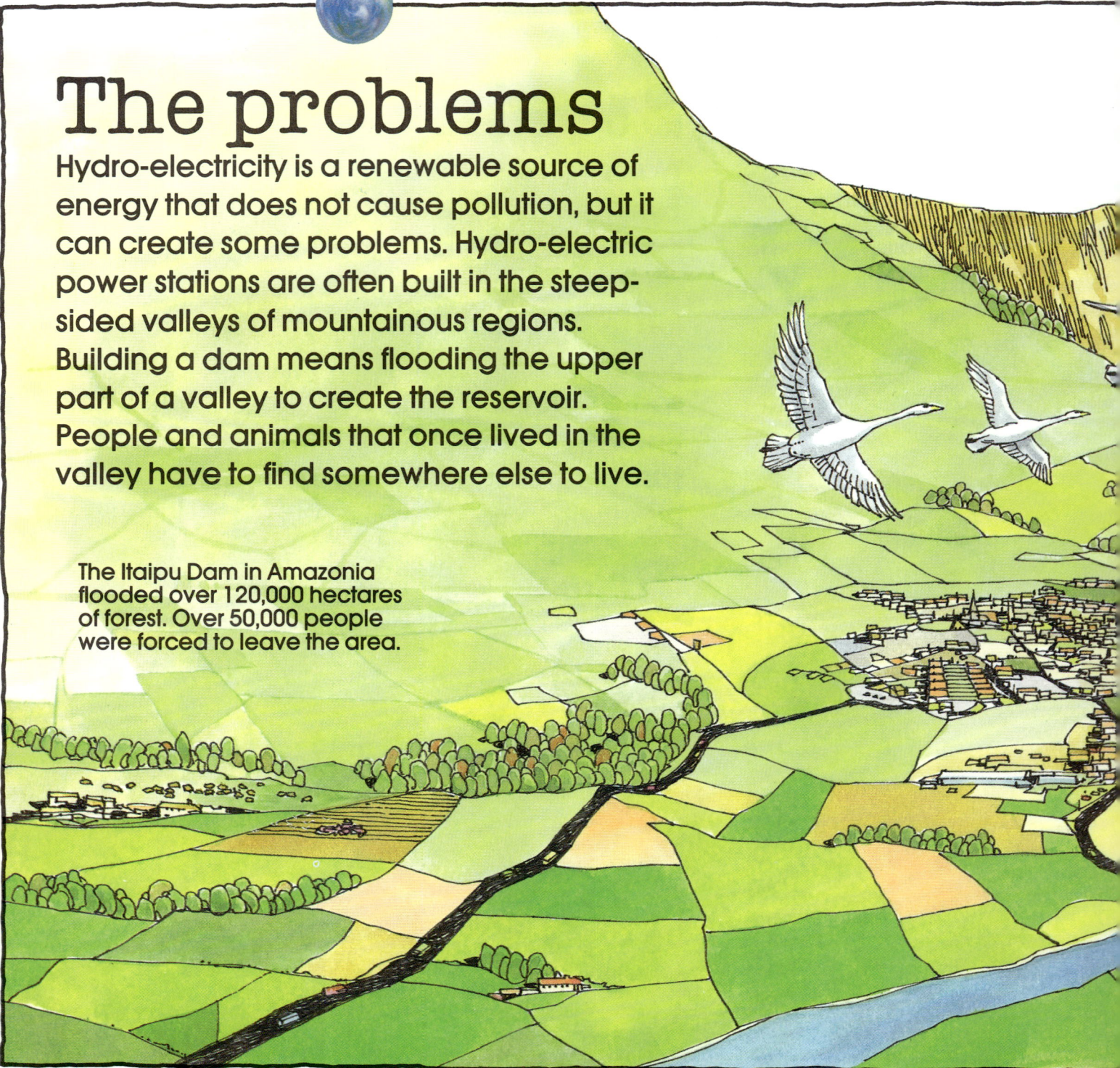

In mountainous regions, there is an added risk of an earthquake or landslide destroying the dam.

Blocking the flow
Mountain streams carry large quantities of silt particles. Silt builds up and blocks the water pipes.

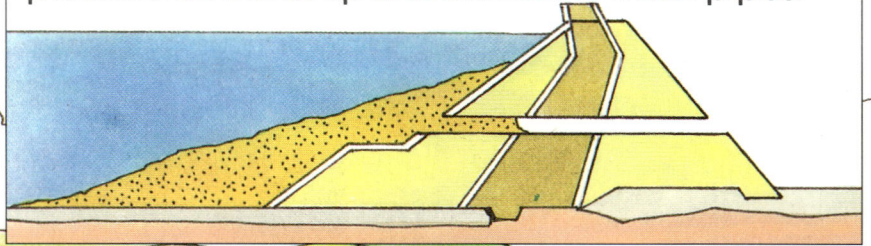

When the Aswan Dam in Egypt was completed, farmers downstream did not have enough water to irrigate their land. Fish in nearby rivers died because the food they needed to survive was no longer being washed down from the River Nile.

Using the tides

Electricity can also be produced by the movement of the tide in a river estuary. When the tide rises, water moves up the estuary. As the tide falls, water moves back down the estuary. This movement can be used to drive turbines in a tidal barrier built across the estuary. The top of the barrier can be used as a bridge. The world's largest tidal power station is situated on the coast of Brittany in France.

The Severn Estuary
In Britain, one of the best places for a tidal power barrier is the Severn Estuary. Several schemes have been proposed for the area, but no decision has yet been made.

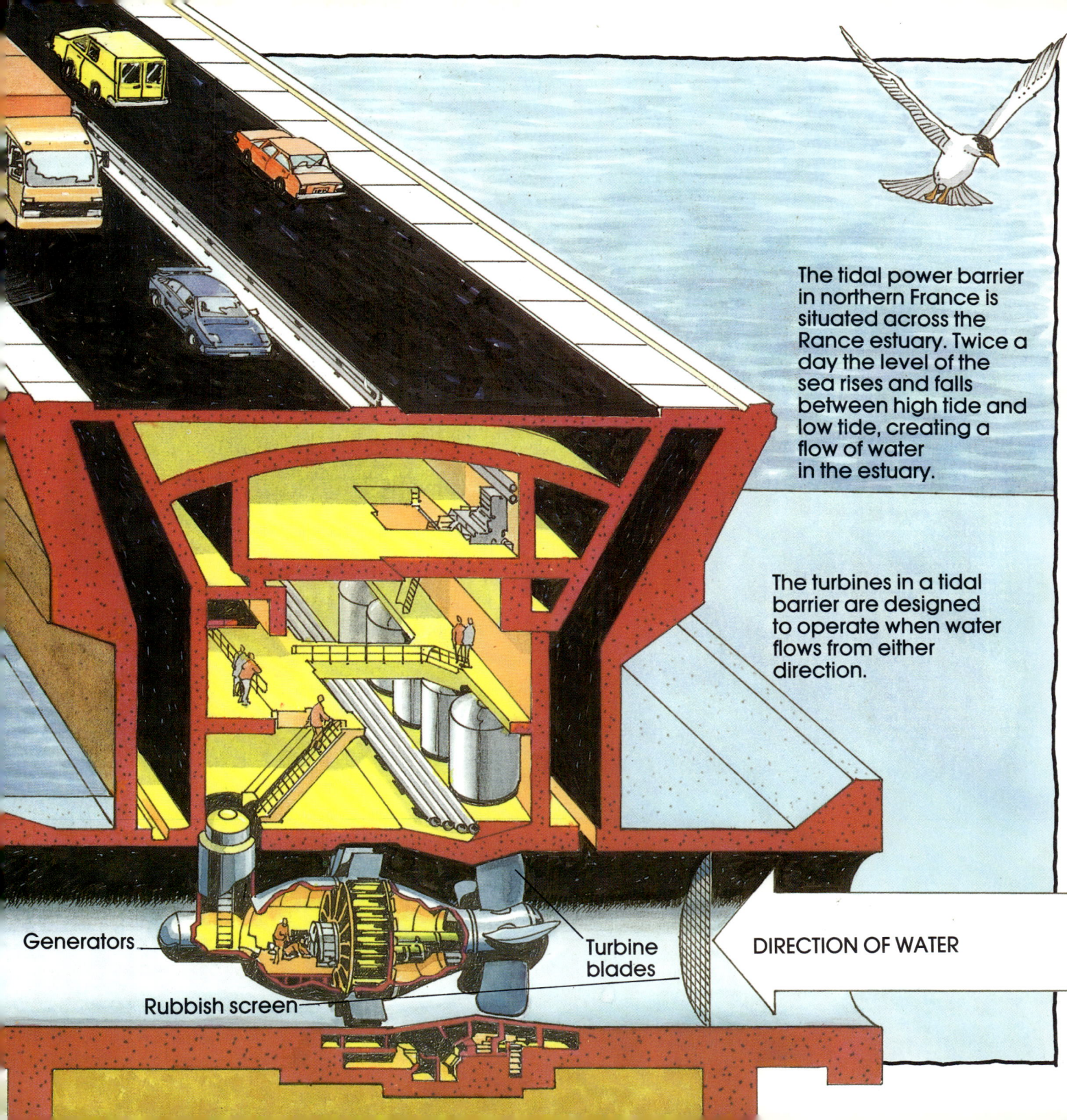

The tidal power barrier in northern France is situated across the Rance estuary. Twice a day the level of the sea rises and falls between high tide and low tide, creating a flow of water in the estuary.

The turbines in a tidal barrier are designed to operate when water flows from either direction.

Generators

Turbine blades

Rubbish screen

DIRECTION OF WATER

Into the future

In future, people will rely more and more on alternative energy sources. Wind turbines and hydro-electric power stations will become more common. Many methods are already being used for collecting the Sun's power. The oceans are the biggest untapped power source on Earth. New machines have been designed that convert the movement of waves into electricity.

Wind farms may be built offshore to reduce the nuisance from noise. Once all the big rivers have been used, people will have to build small hydro-electric power stations to supply individual communities.

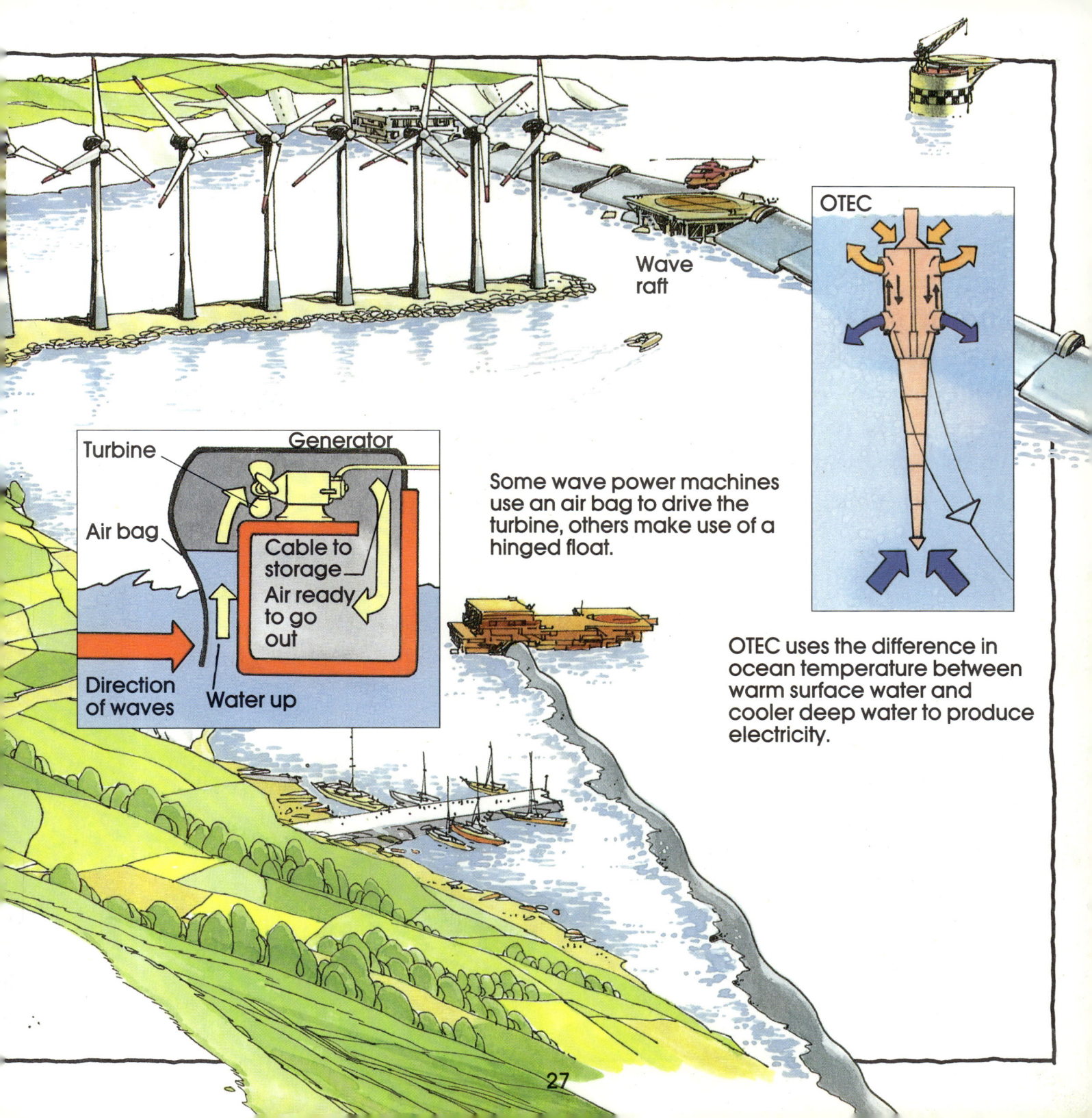

OTEC

Wave raft

Turbine **Generator**

Air bag

Cable to storage

Air ready to go out

Direction of waves

Water up

Some wave power machines use an air bag to drive the turbine, others make use of a hinged float.

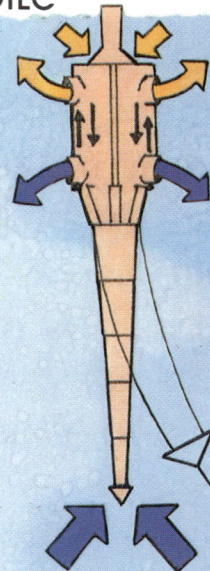

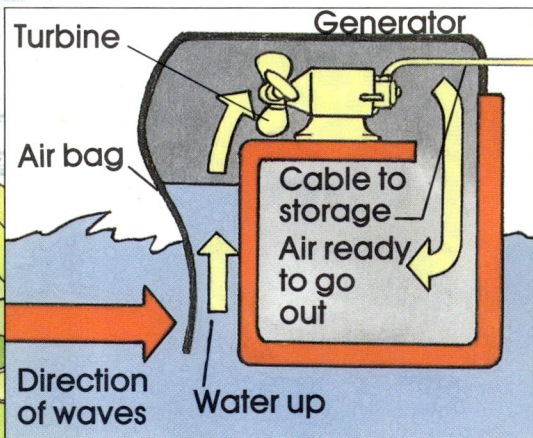

OTEC uses the difference in ocean temperature between warm surface water and cooler deep water to produce electricity.

Fact file

The first recorded windmills were built in Iran during the 7th century. This new invention spread slowly, and windmills were not built in Europe until the 10th century. The first wind turbines for making electricity were constructed in Denmark at the end of the 19th century.

The tide was also used to turn conventional waterwheels in tide mills. As the tide rose it filled a reservoir and was trapped behind heavy wooden gates. Then the water was allowed to flow out and turn the wheel. As well as grinding corn, this rotation movement could be used to blow air into the furnaces where iron was made. The use of waterwheels in industry was gradually replaced by steam engines. However, some working waterwheels can still be found today. Most towns and villages had a mill, which was situated close to a fast-flowing river or tidal estuary.

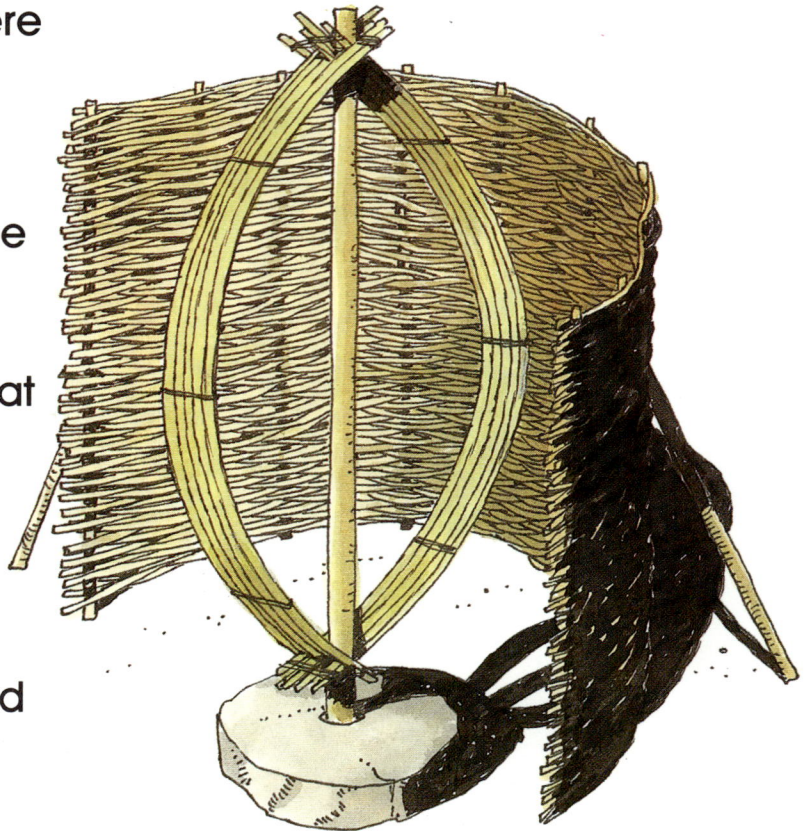

The world's largest concrete dam is the Grand Coulee dam in the United States, which was opened in 1942. The Grand Coulee is more than 1.2 kilometres long, and measures 167 metres in height. The dam is the largest structure ever made of concrete and it weighs more than 19 million tonnes.

Waterwheels were once essential for any large town or city. They were often built into the city walls, and supplied the inhabitants with flour to bake bread. Waterwheels mounted on river boats once saved the city of Rome from starvation during a seige.

Wind turbines produce much more energy than windmills. A traditional windmill produces about as much energy as 200 human workers. A modern wind turbine can produce as much of energy as 60,000 workers. The map below shows the world's windiest areas, which include areas near the coast and islands.

Wind and water can also be used to provide electricity in remote districts. In the town of Montesalvado, Peru, the school has its own "micro" hydro-electric power station. A small turbine, which has been specially designed so as not to spoil the environment, produces all the electricity that the school needs.

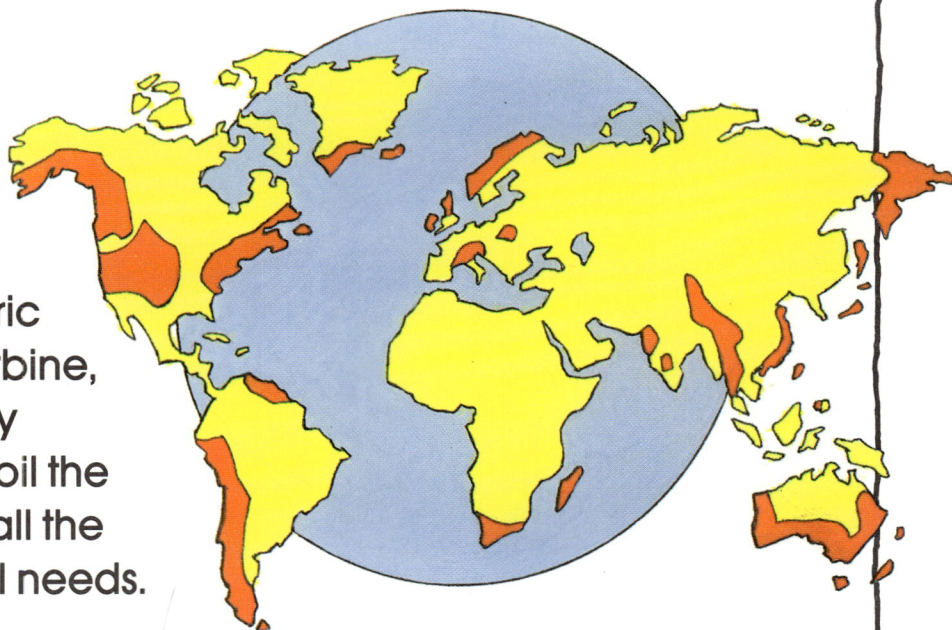

Glossary

Estuary
The wide part of a river where it runs into the sea.

Fossil fuel
Coal, oil or gas are the remains of living things, such as plants or animals, which have been trapped or buried underground for thousands of years. When these fuels are burned, they release this trapped energy as heat.

Generator
A machine that converts rotation into electricity.

Global warming
The name given to the gradual warming up of the Earth's atmosphere as a result of burning too many fossil fuels.

Hydro-electricity
Electricity produced from the flow of water.

Rotation
A turning movement.

Turbine
A machine that converts straight line movement (e.g. the wind or the flow of water) into rotation.

Waterwheel
One of the earliest and simplest forms of water turbine.

Wind turbine
A modern windmill that is used to produce electricity.

Wind farm
An area of land that contains many wind turbines.

Index